MEXICAN VACATION
VIVA MEXICO!

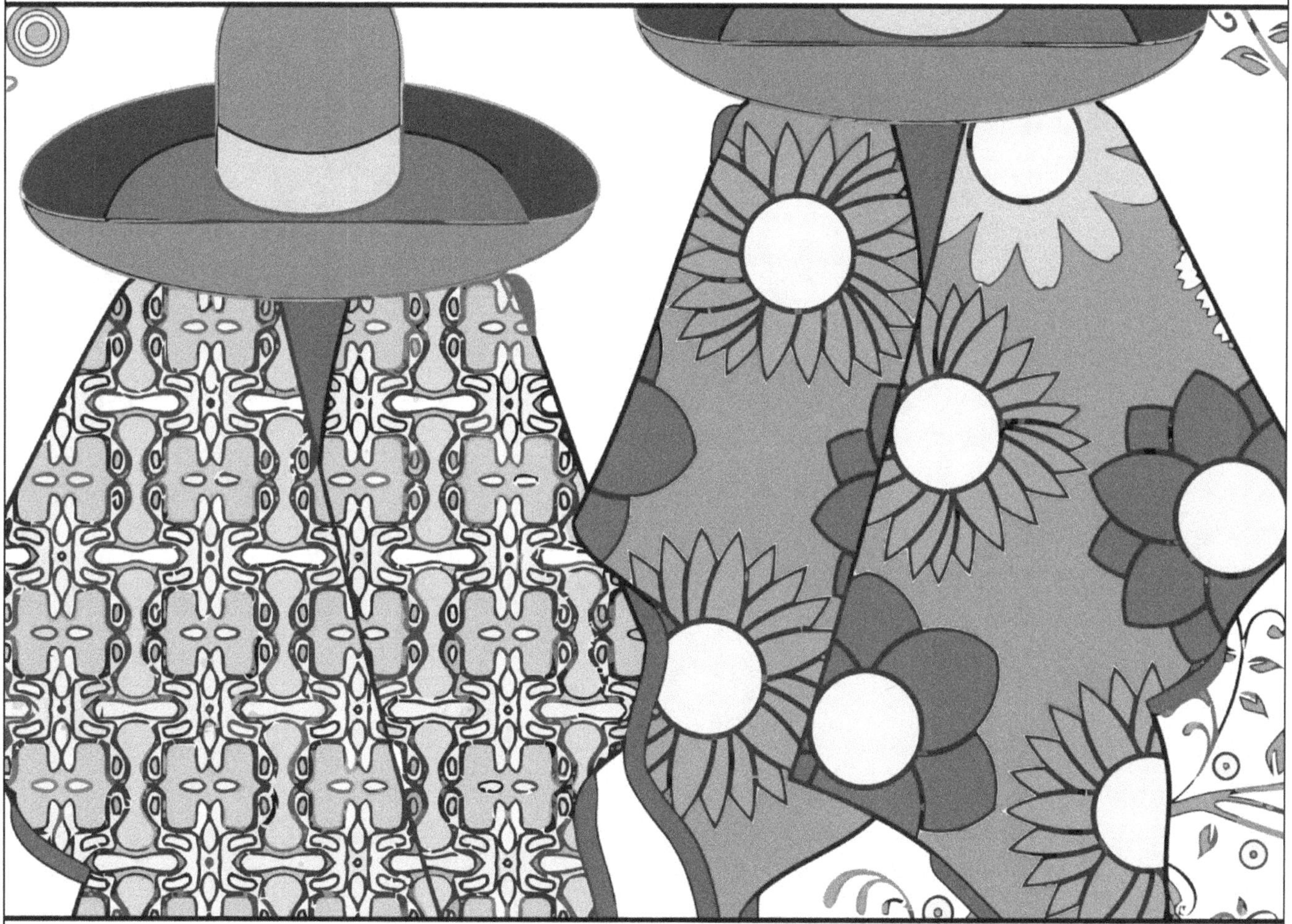

COLORING BOOKS FOR ADULTS

CLIPPEE COLORING BOOKS
BY JAKE WIDMER

Mexican Vacation: Viva Mexico! Coloring Books for Adults

Clippee Coloring
By Jake Widmer

PUBLISHED BY:
Jake Widmer
Copyright © 2015

_____

How to Use This Book

1) Open the book.

_____

2) Turn off the TV.

_____

3) Turn on your favorite relaxing music.

_____

4) Pull out your favorite coloring pencils, crayons, or markers.

_____

5) Dont answer that phone! In fact, put it away! ☺

_____

6) Use your imagination and start coloring!

_____

7) If you feel you've had enough, pick up where you left off at a later time…

_____

8) If you haven't had enough… keep going!

_____

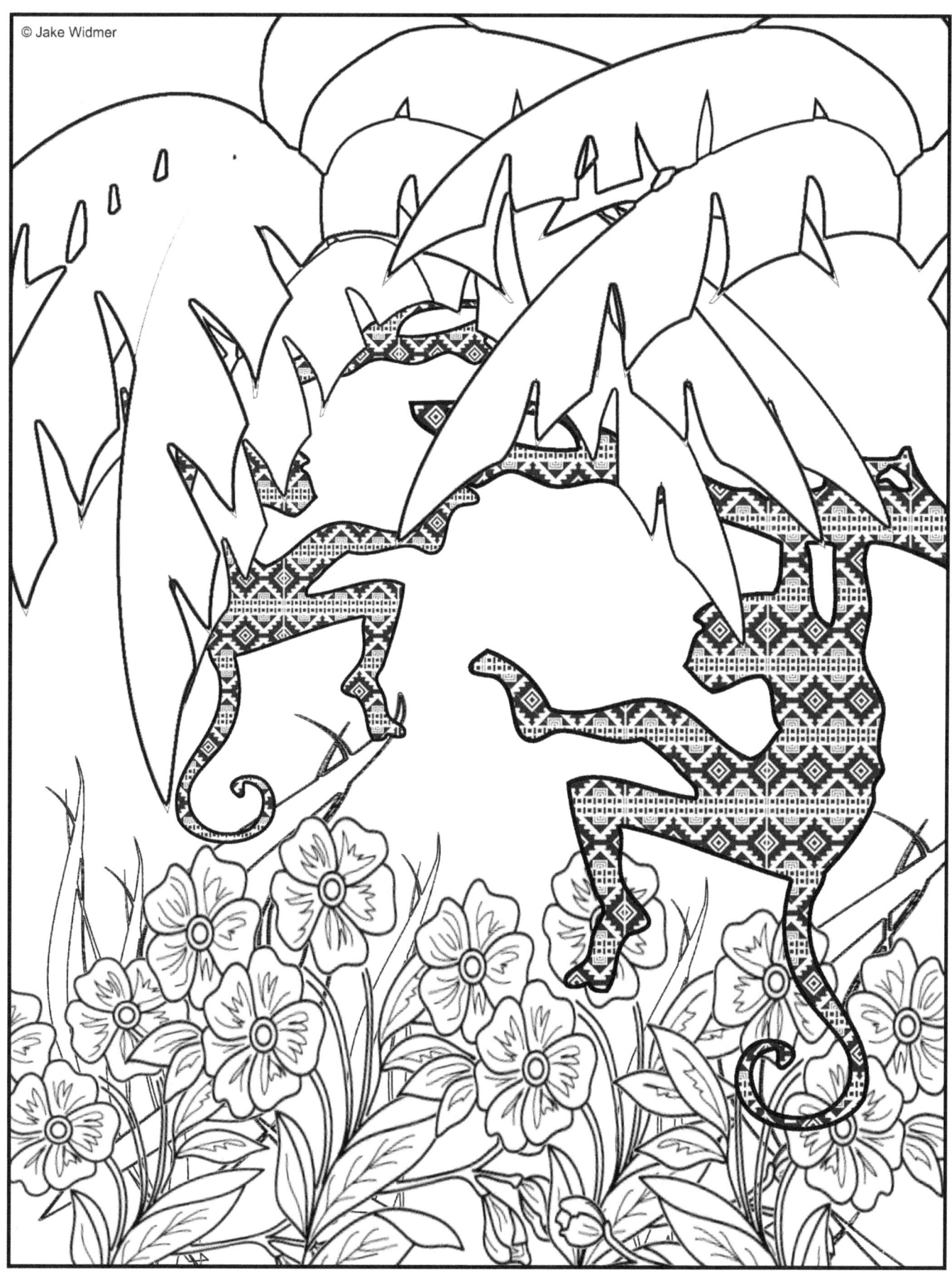

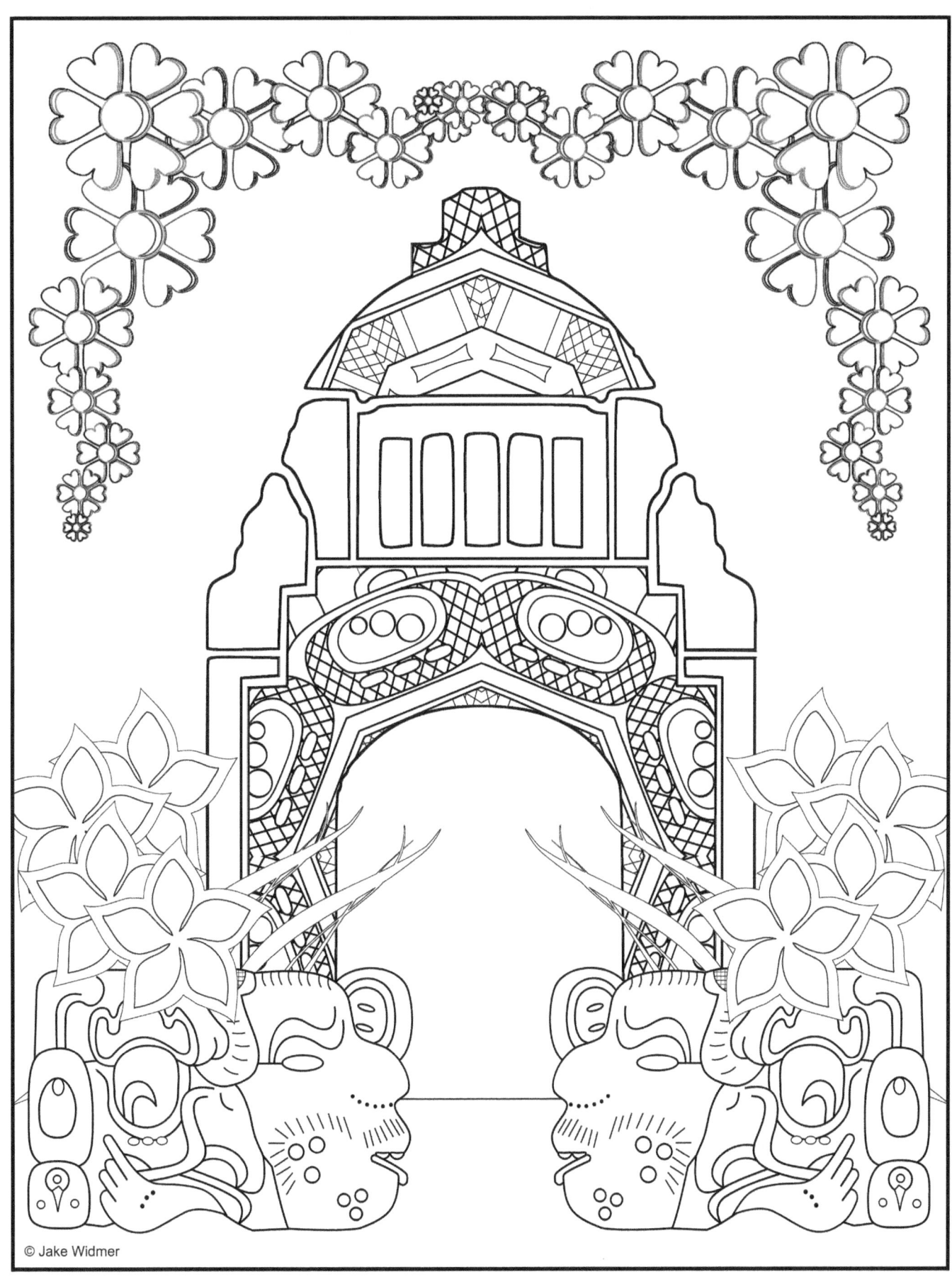

© Jake Widmer

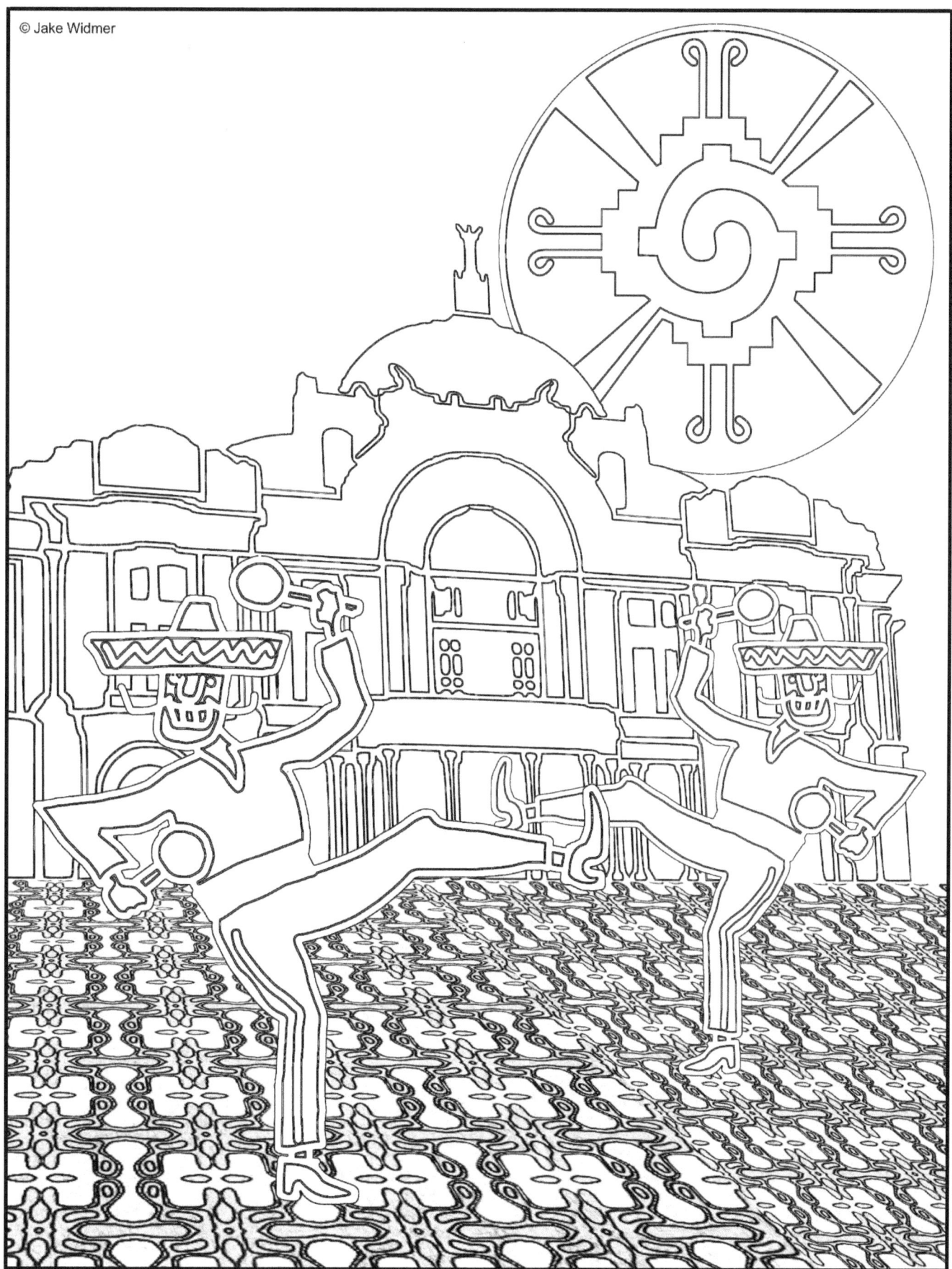

© Jake Widmer

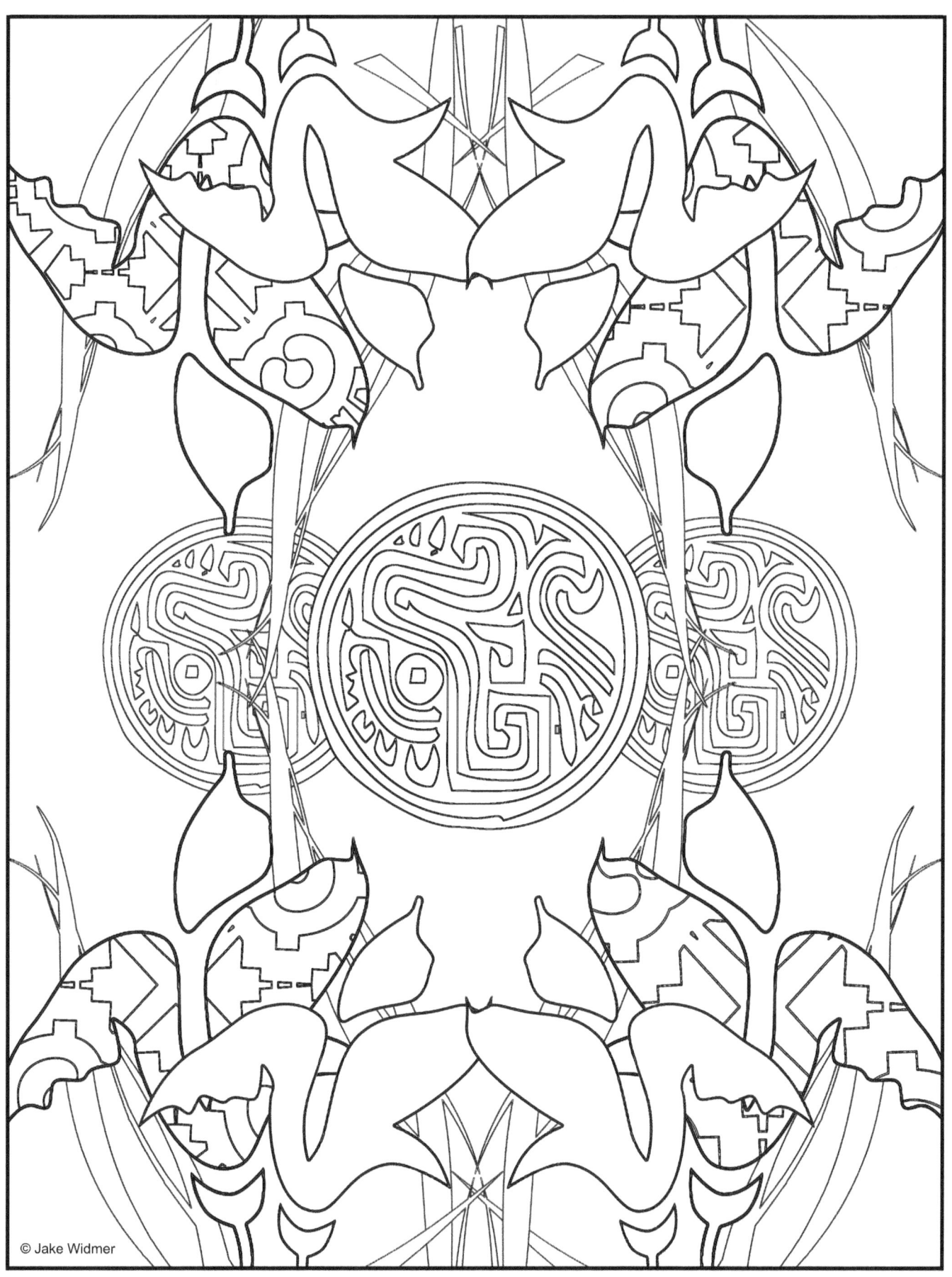

© Jake Widmer

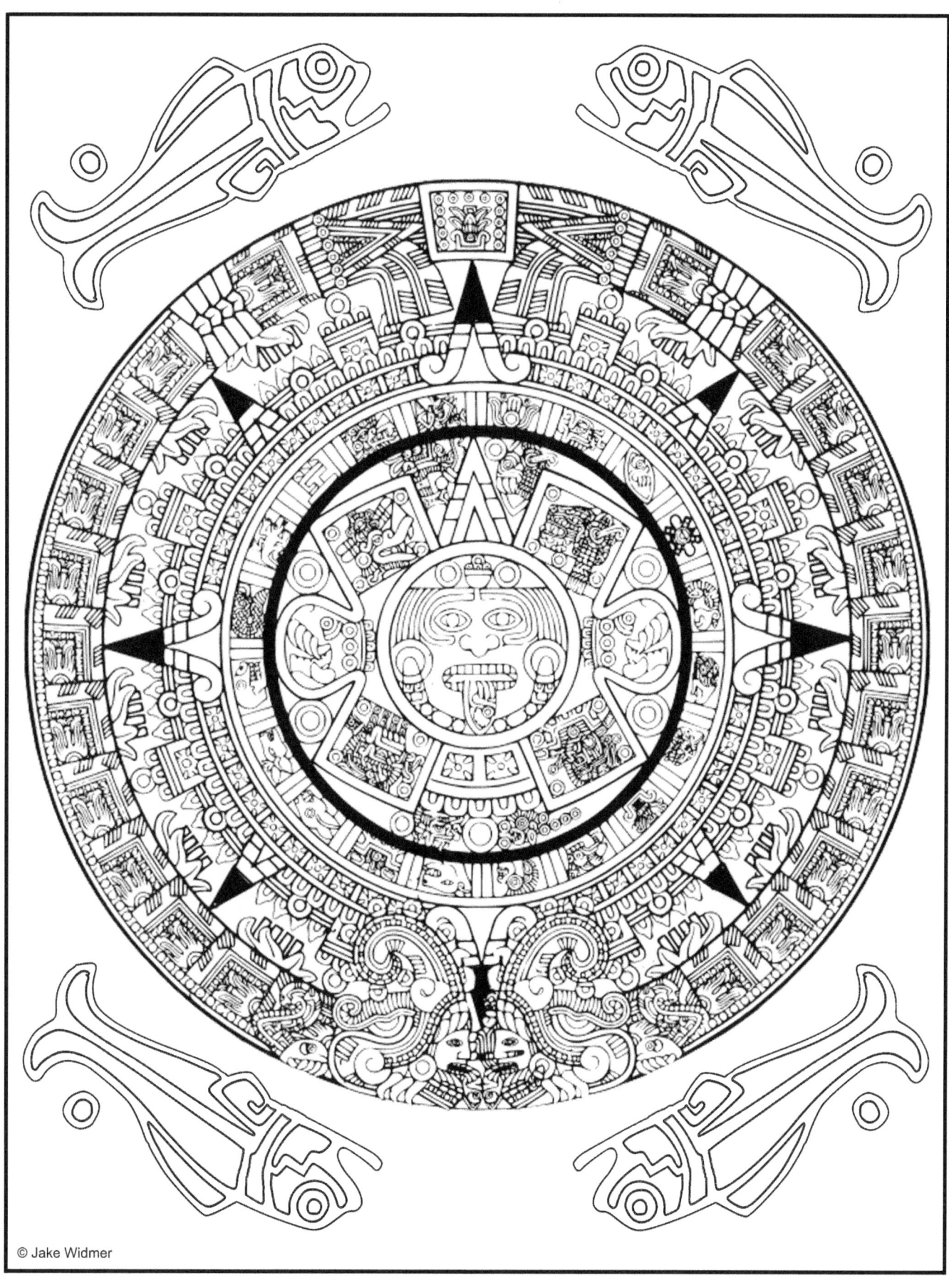

© Jake Widmer

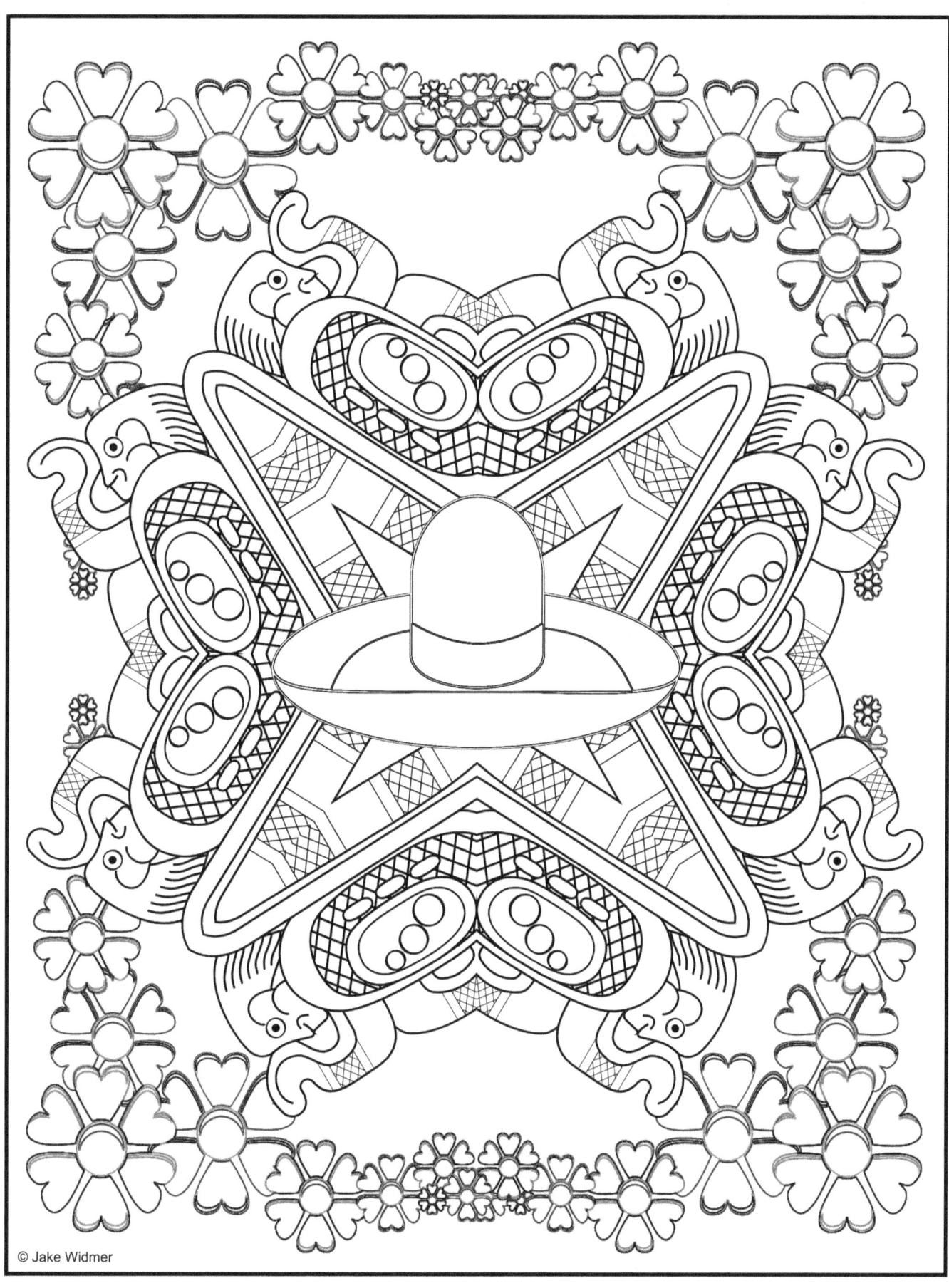

© Jake Widmer

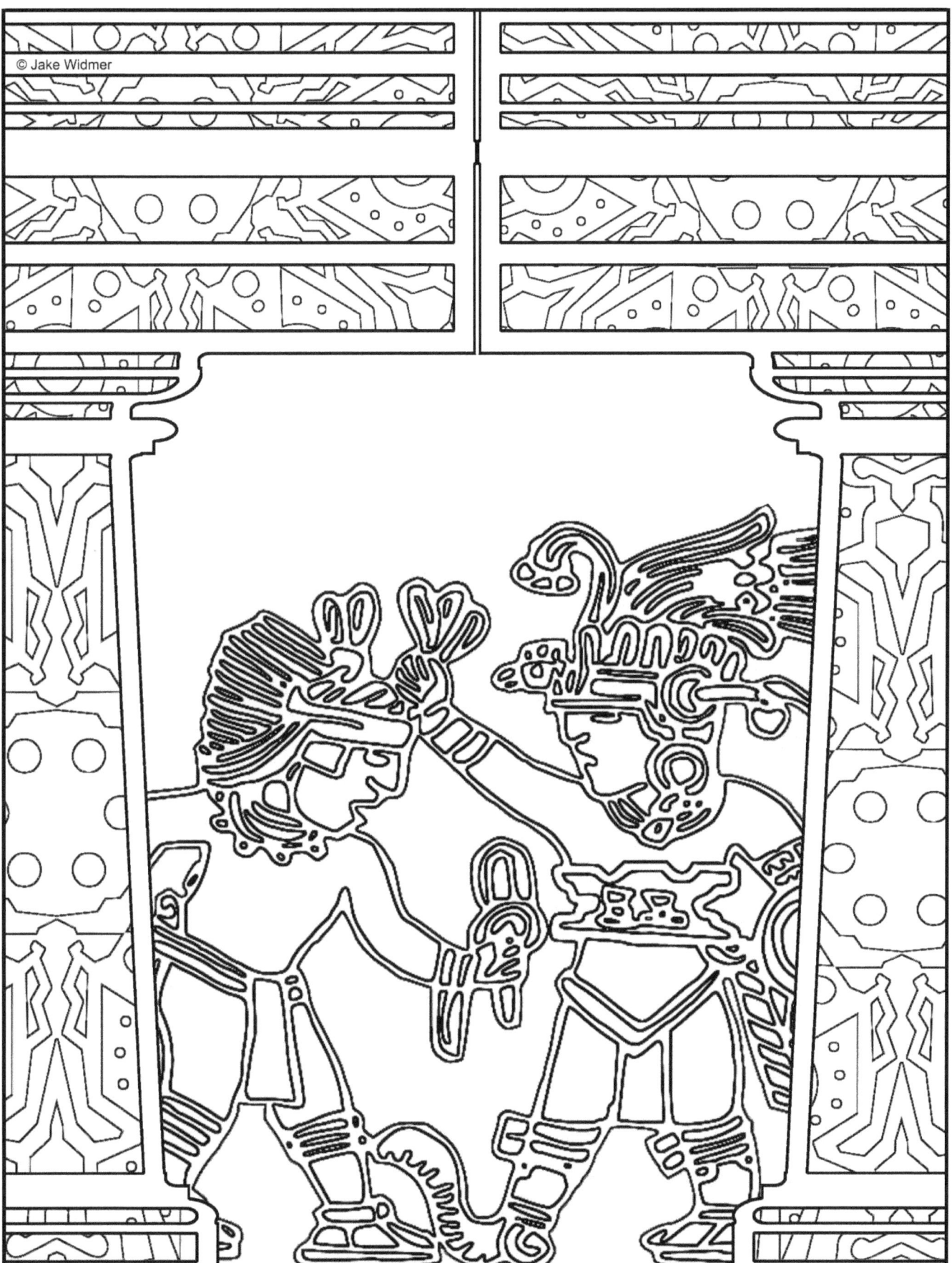

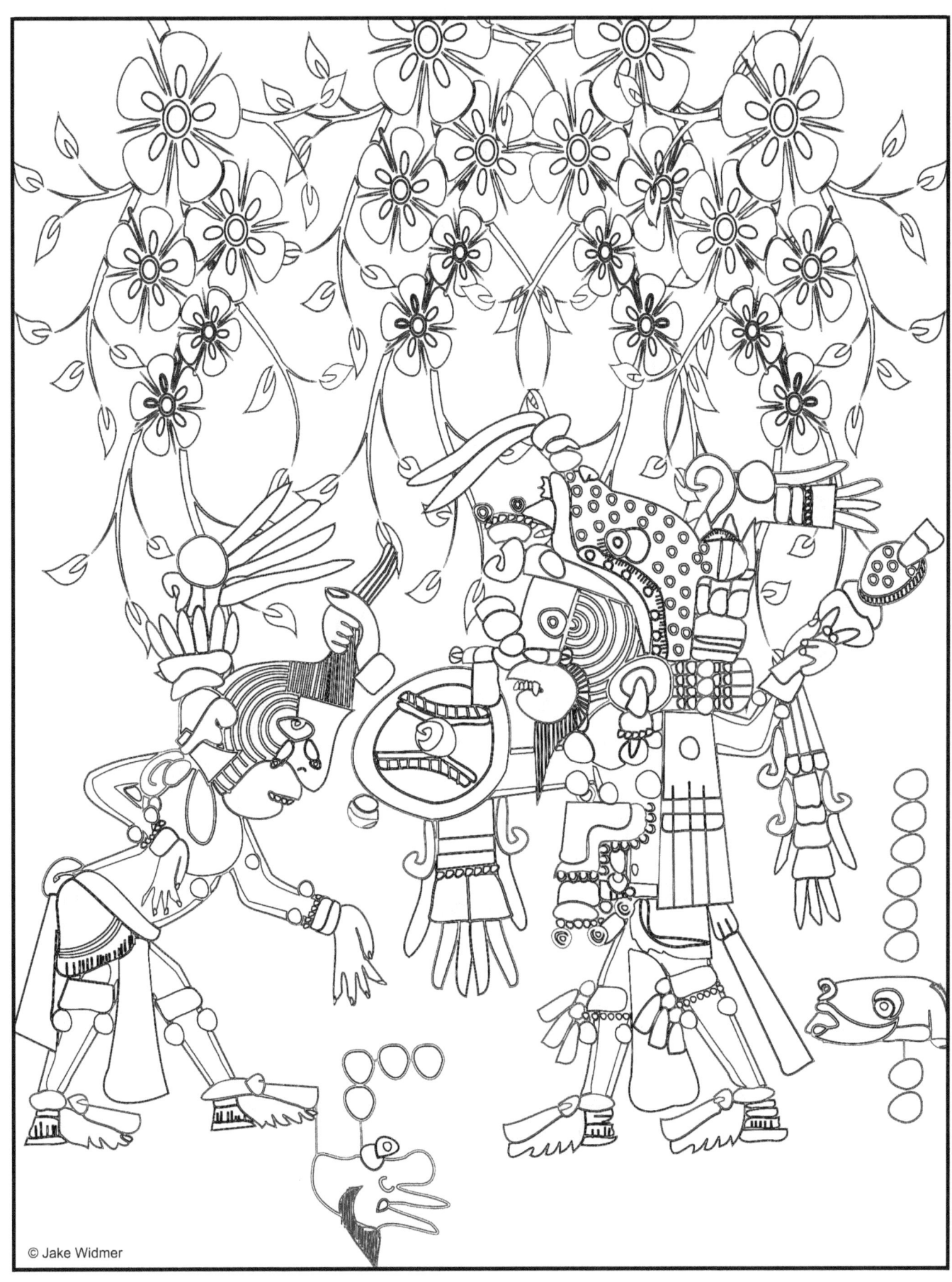

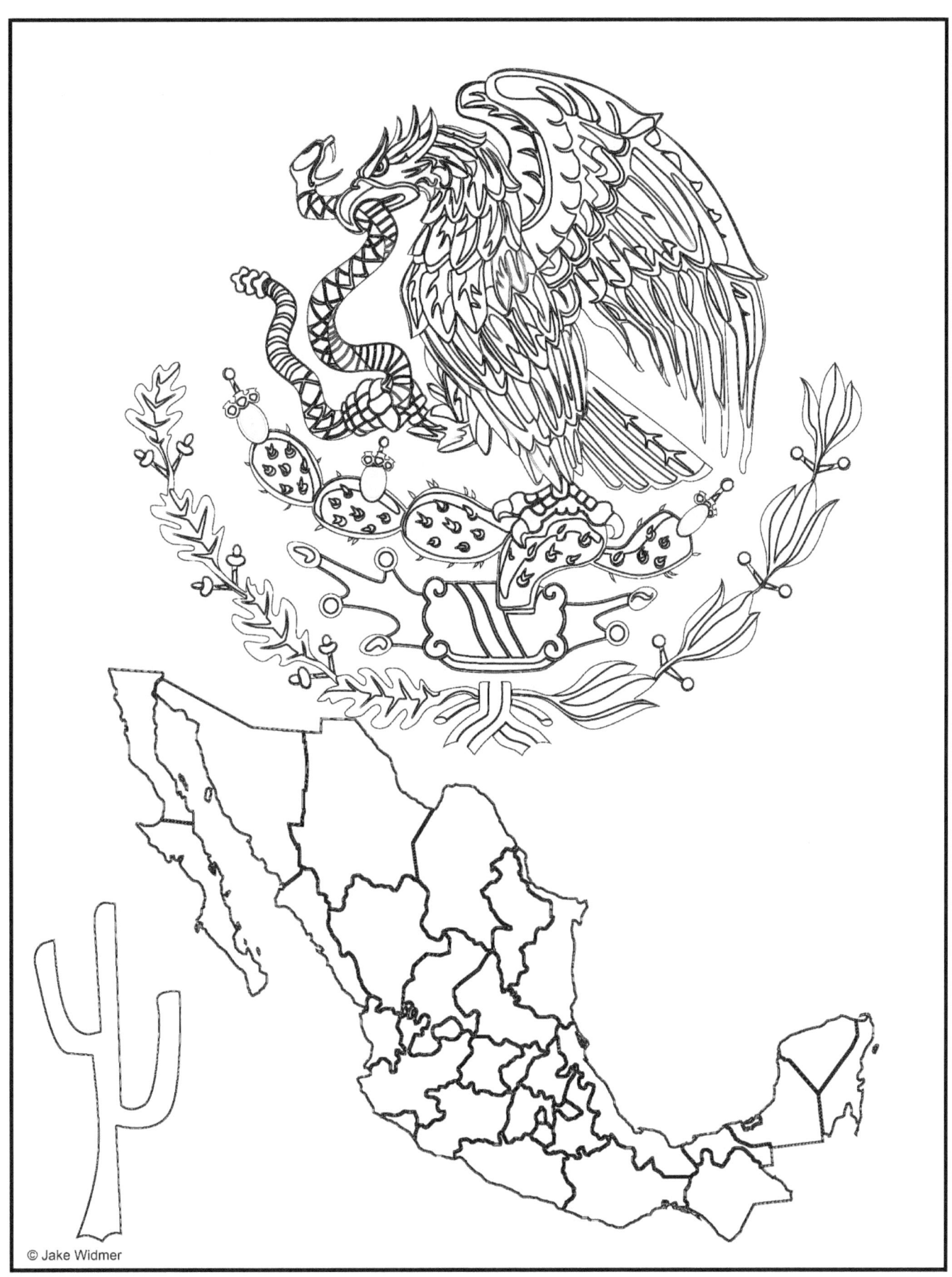

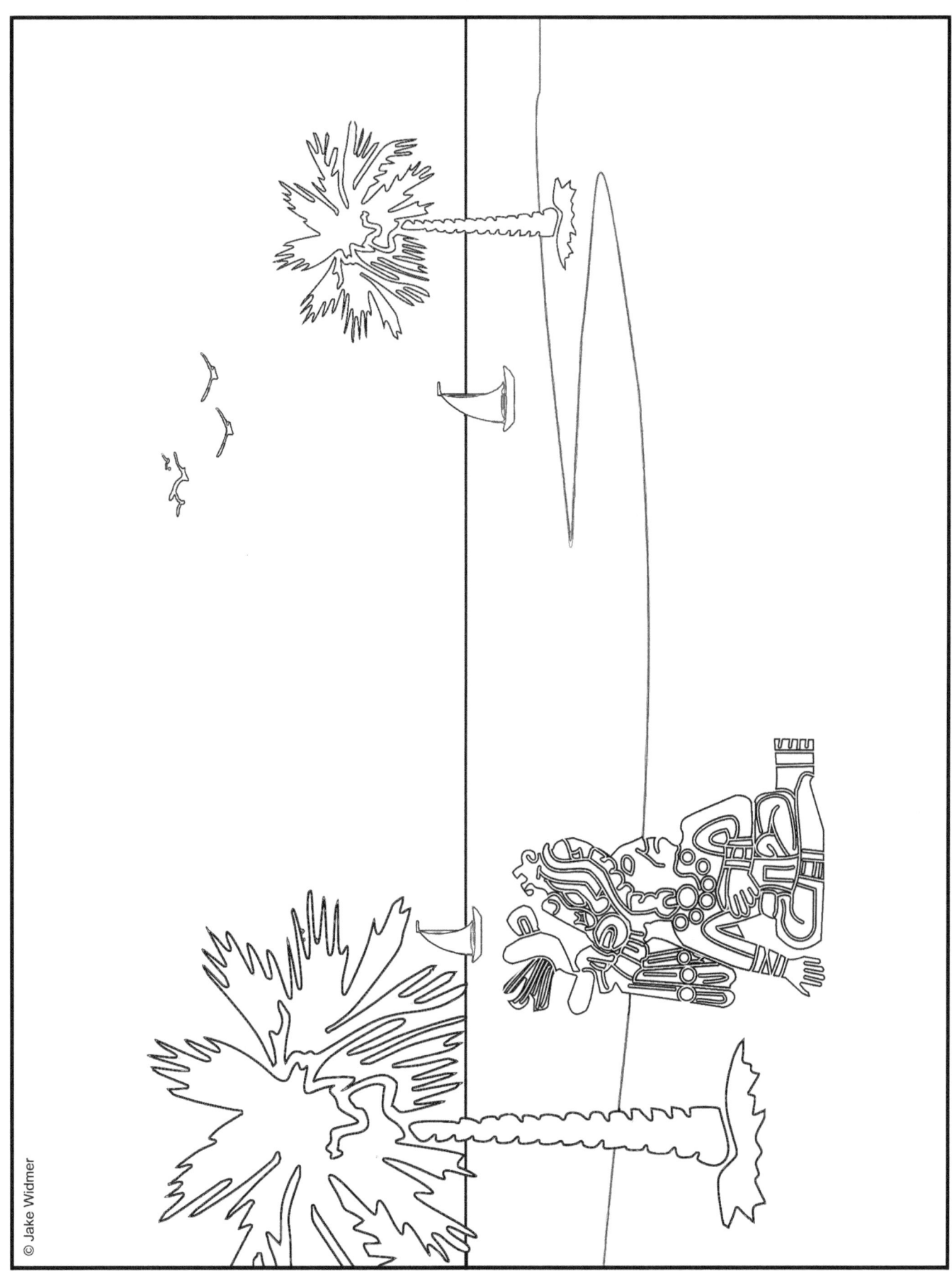

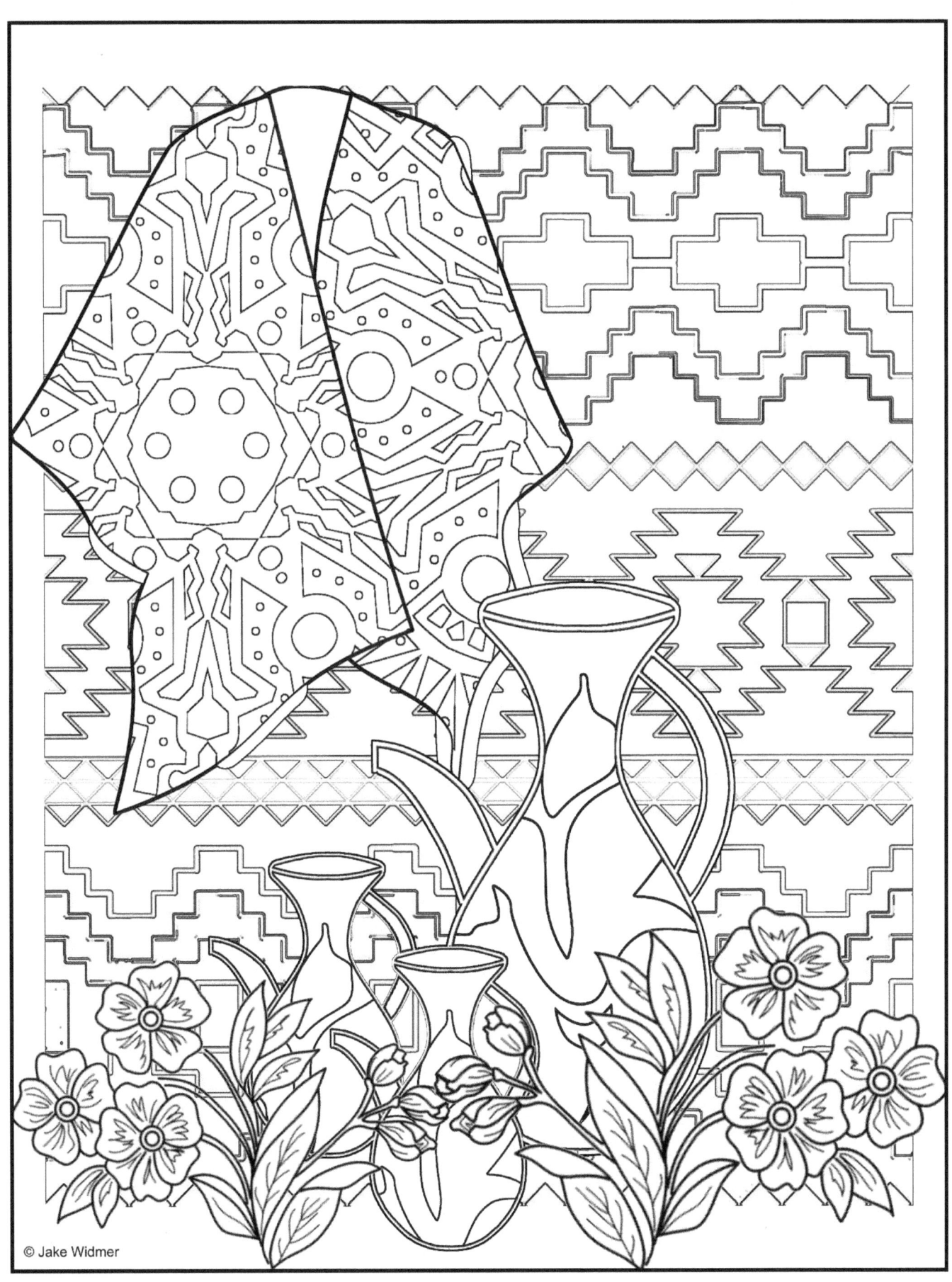

© Jake Widmer

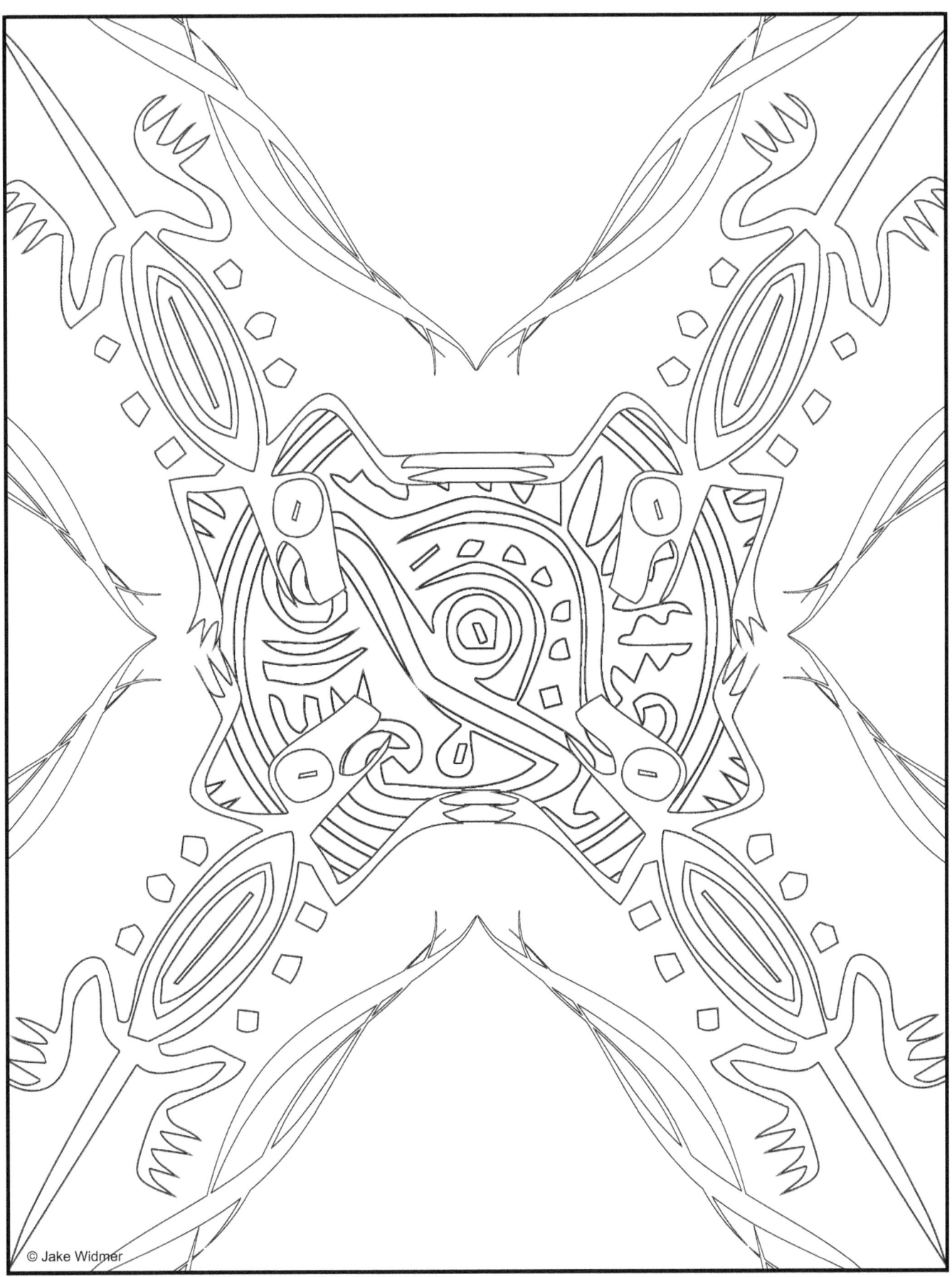

© Jake Widmer

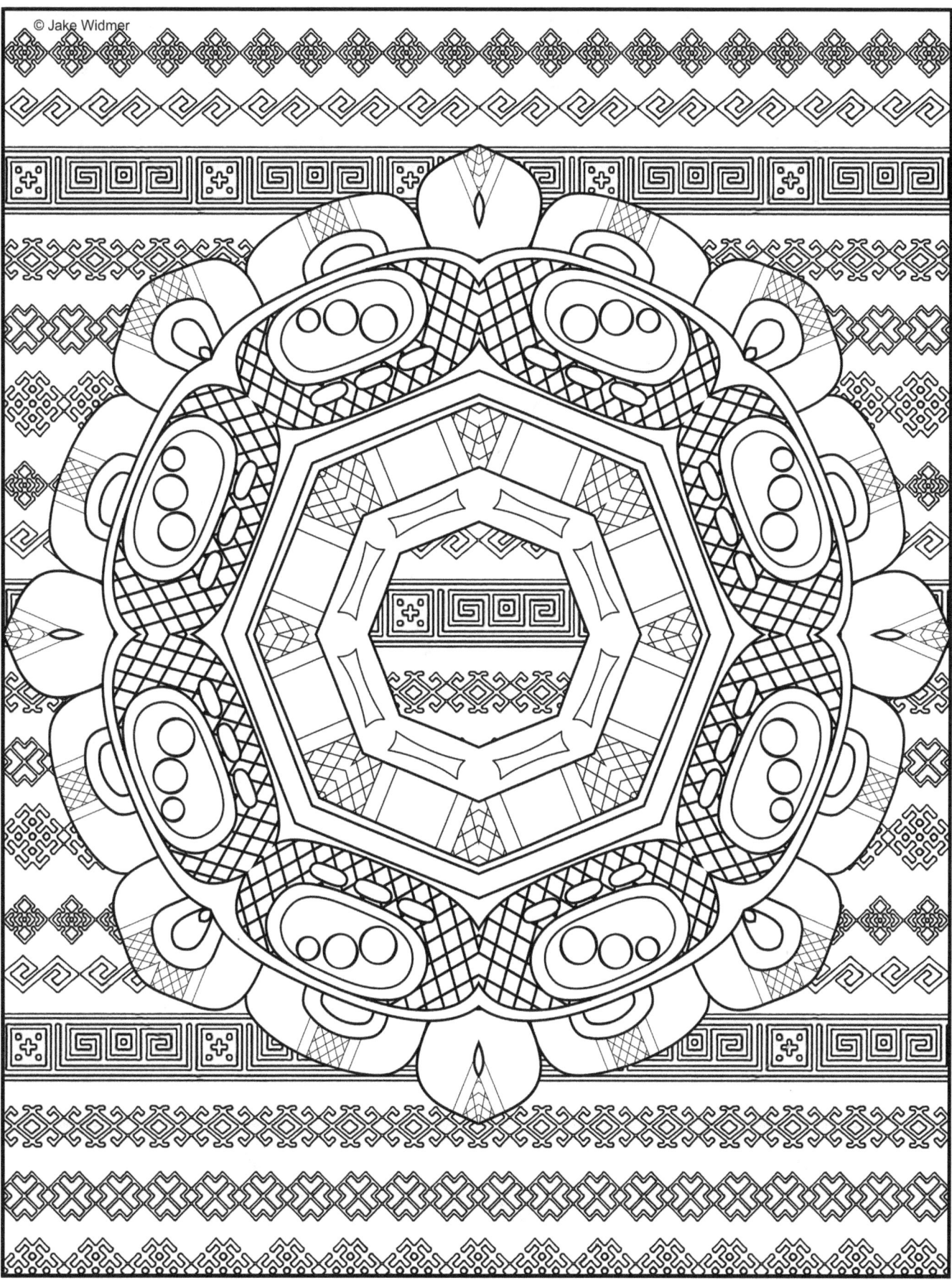

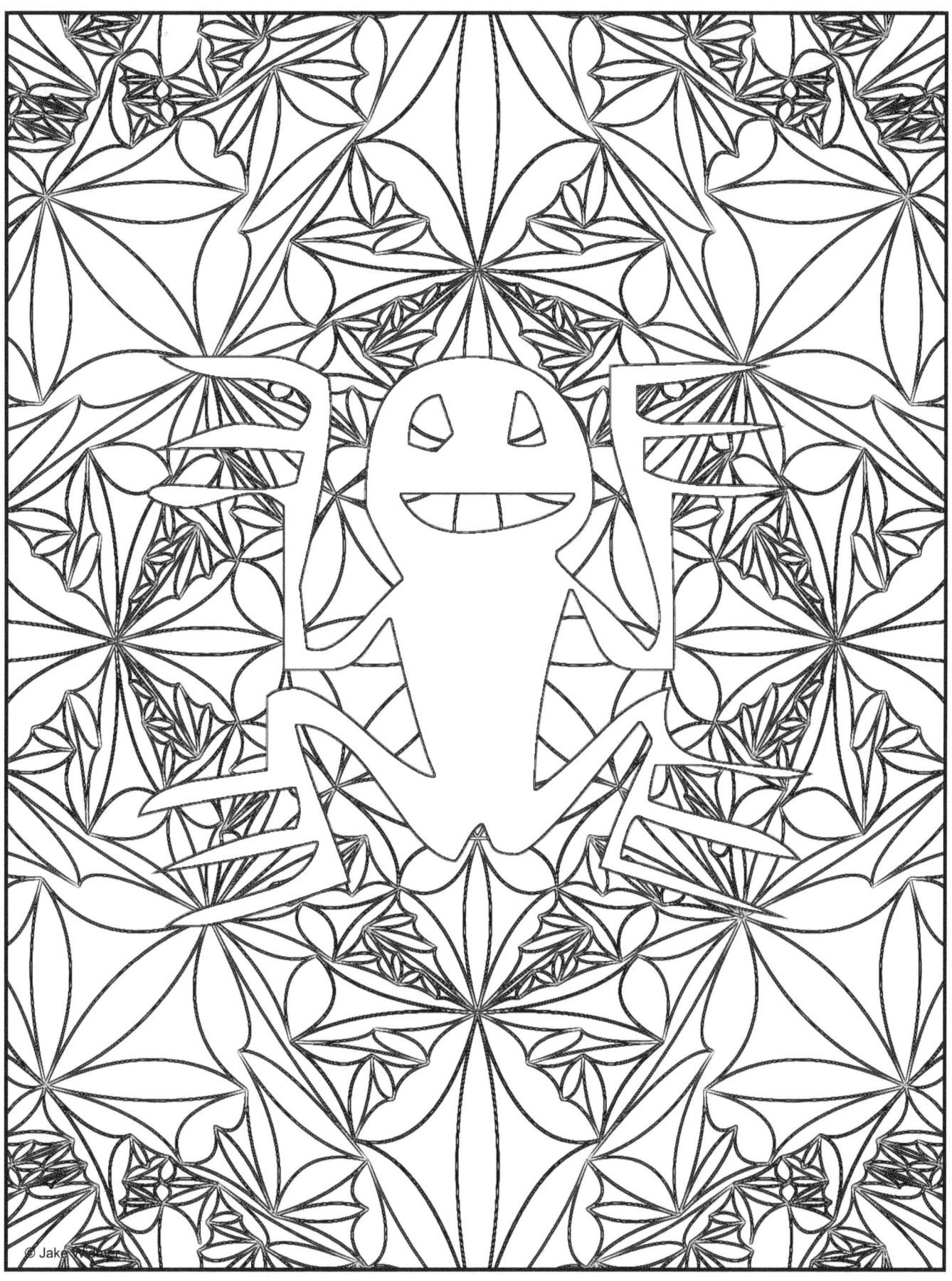

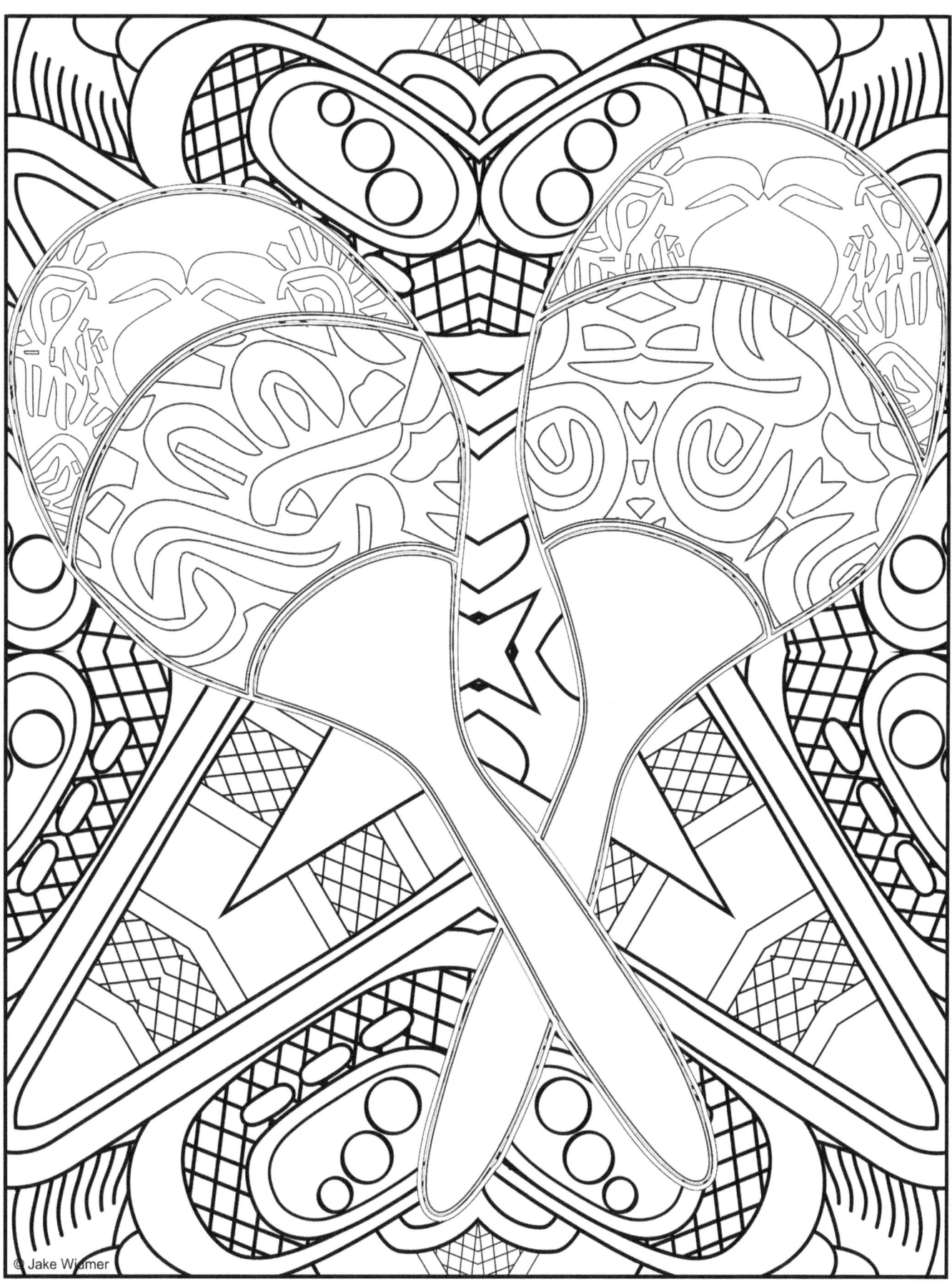

© Jake Widmer

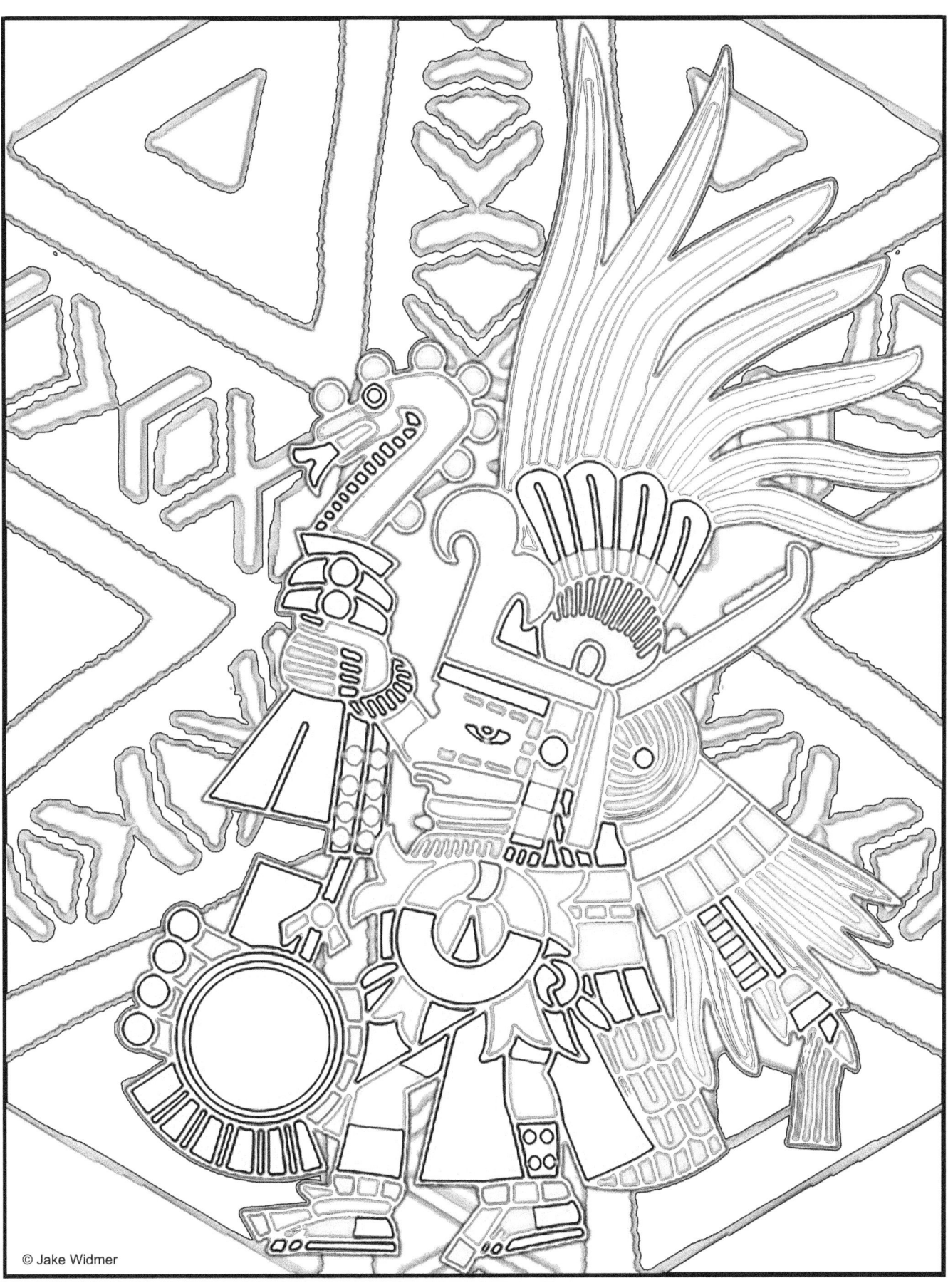

© Jake Widmer

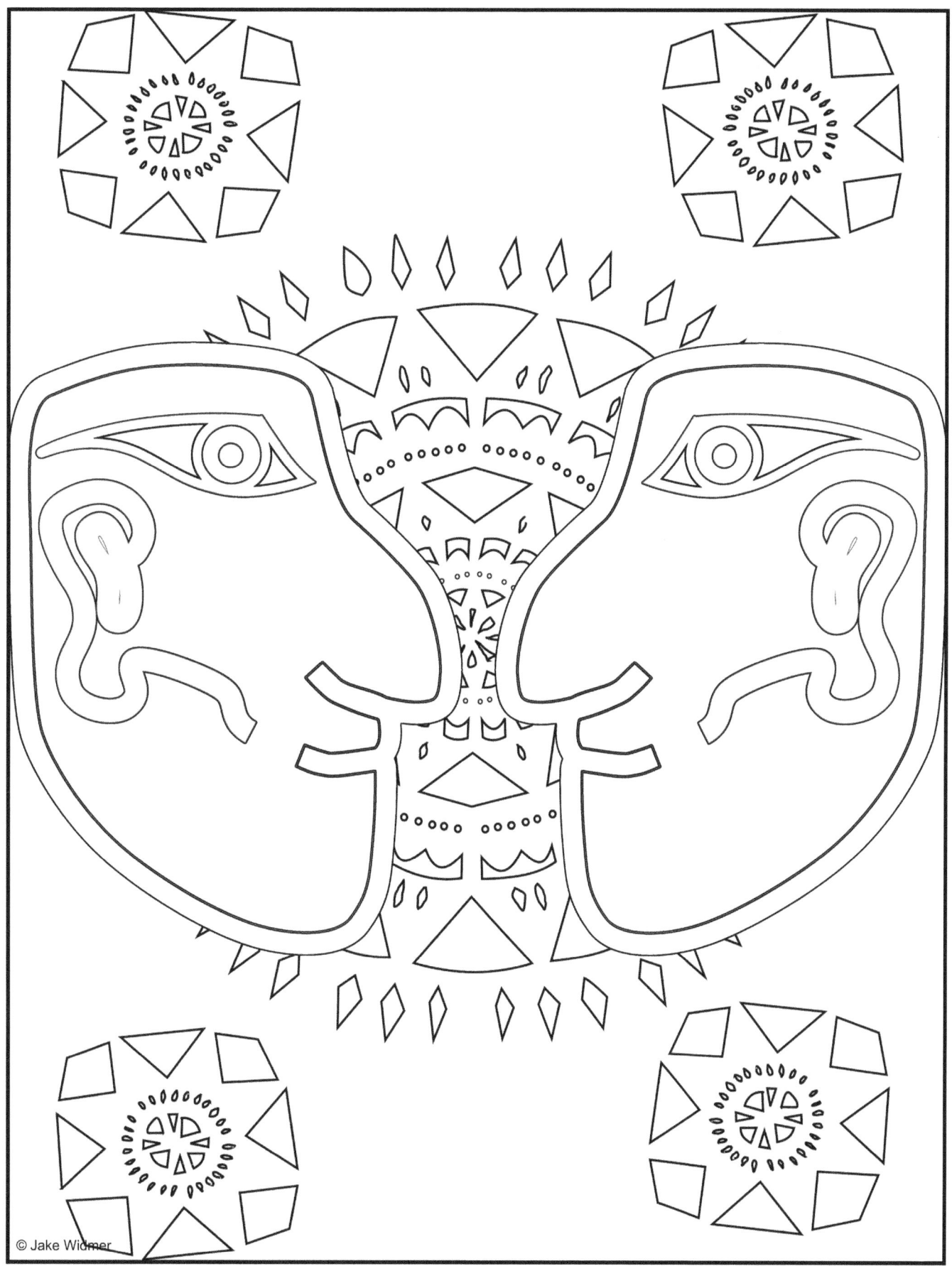

© Jake Widmer

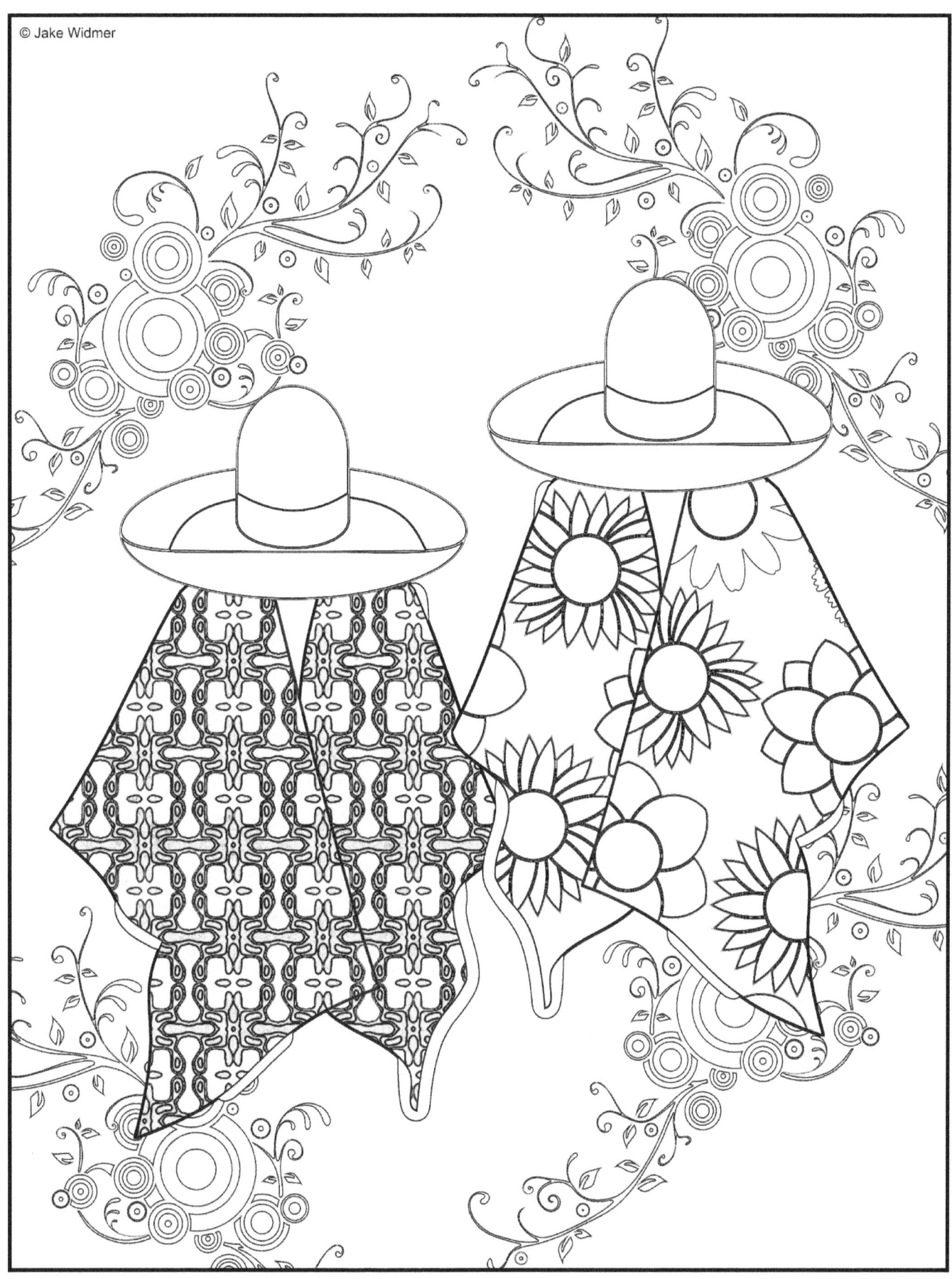

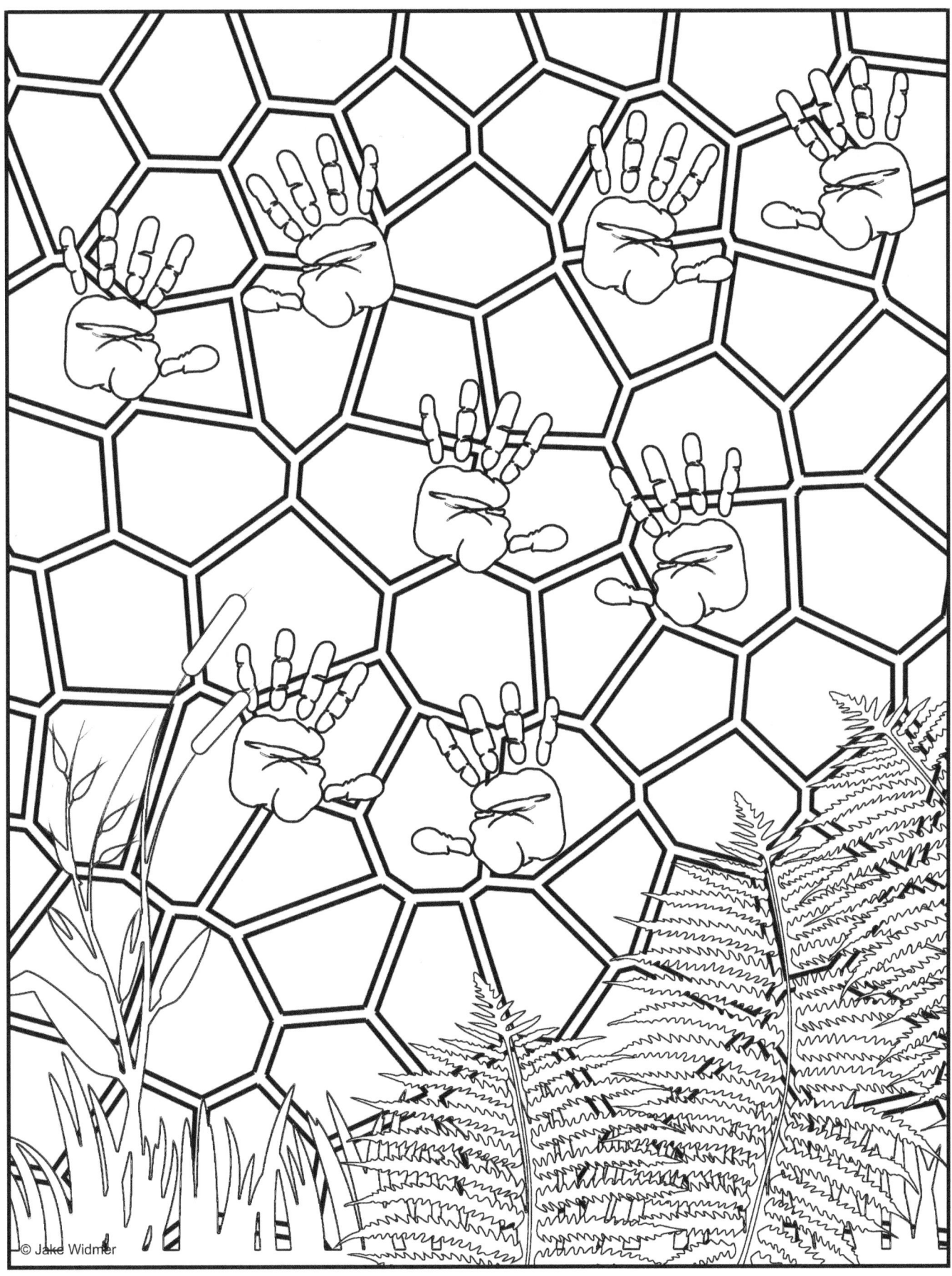

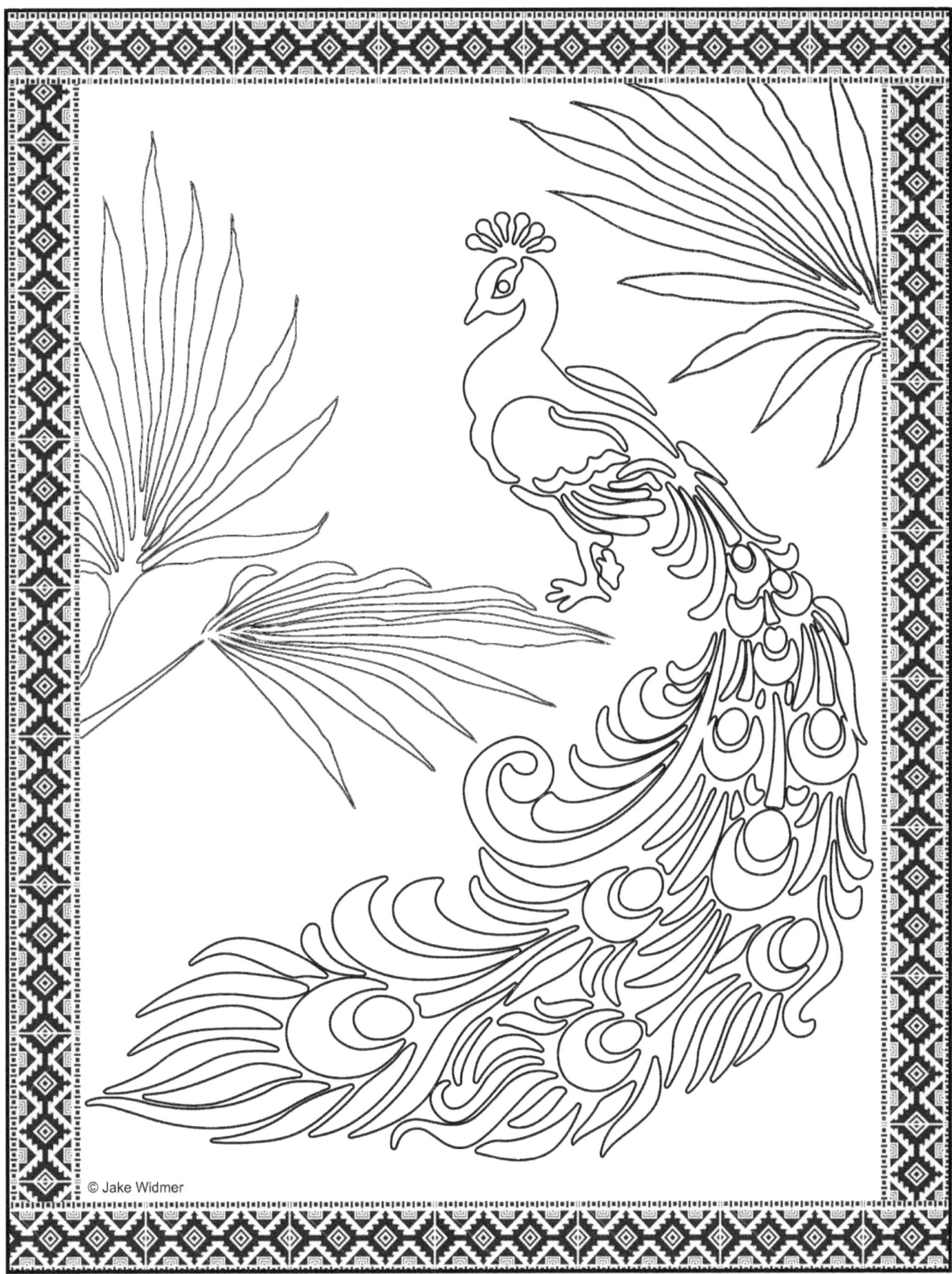

© Jake Widmer

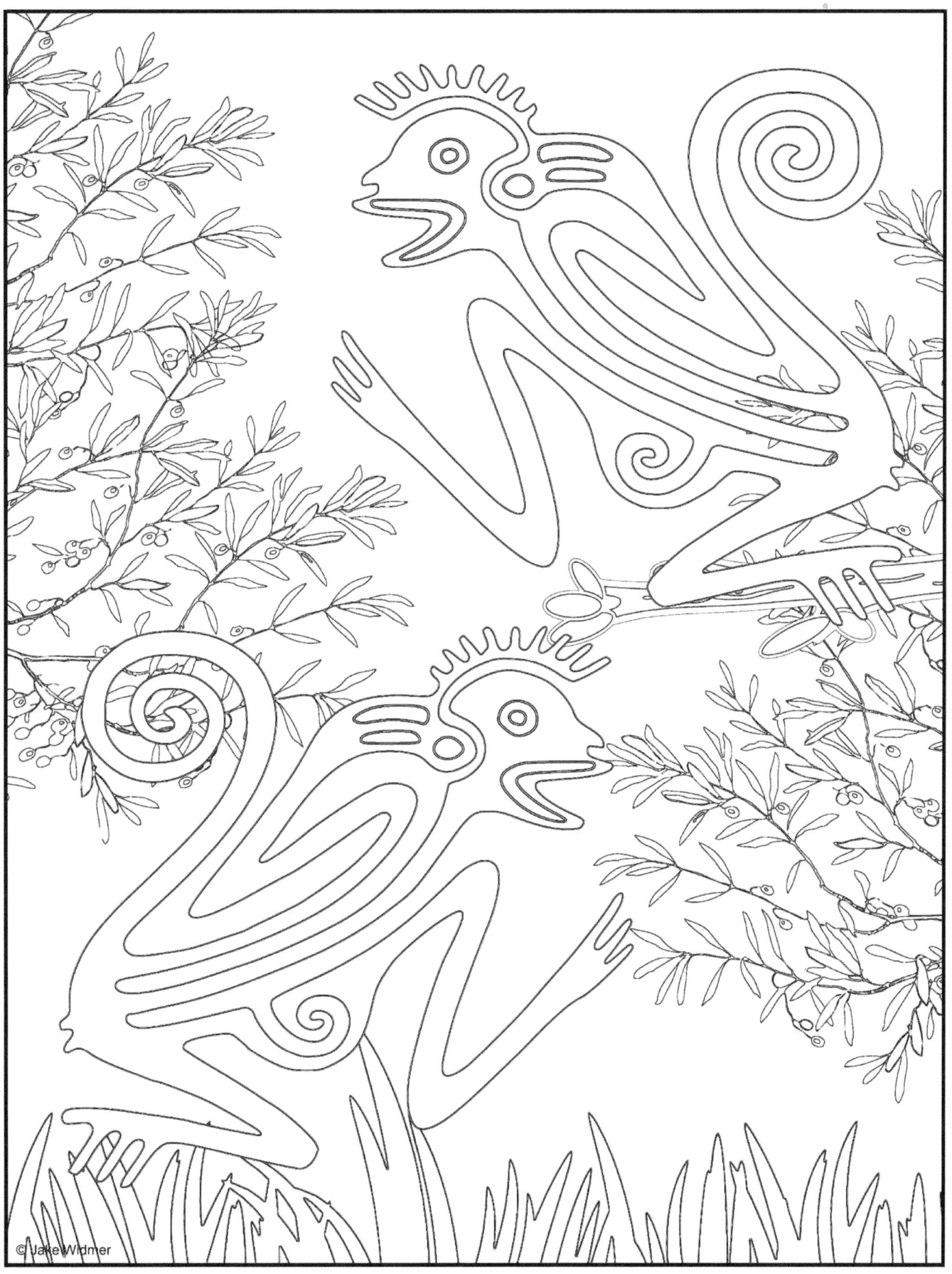

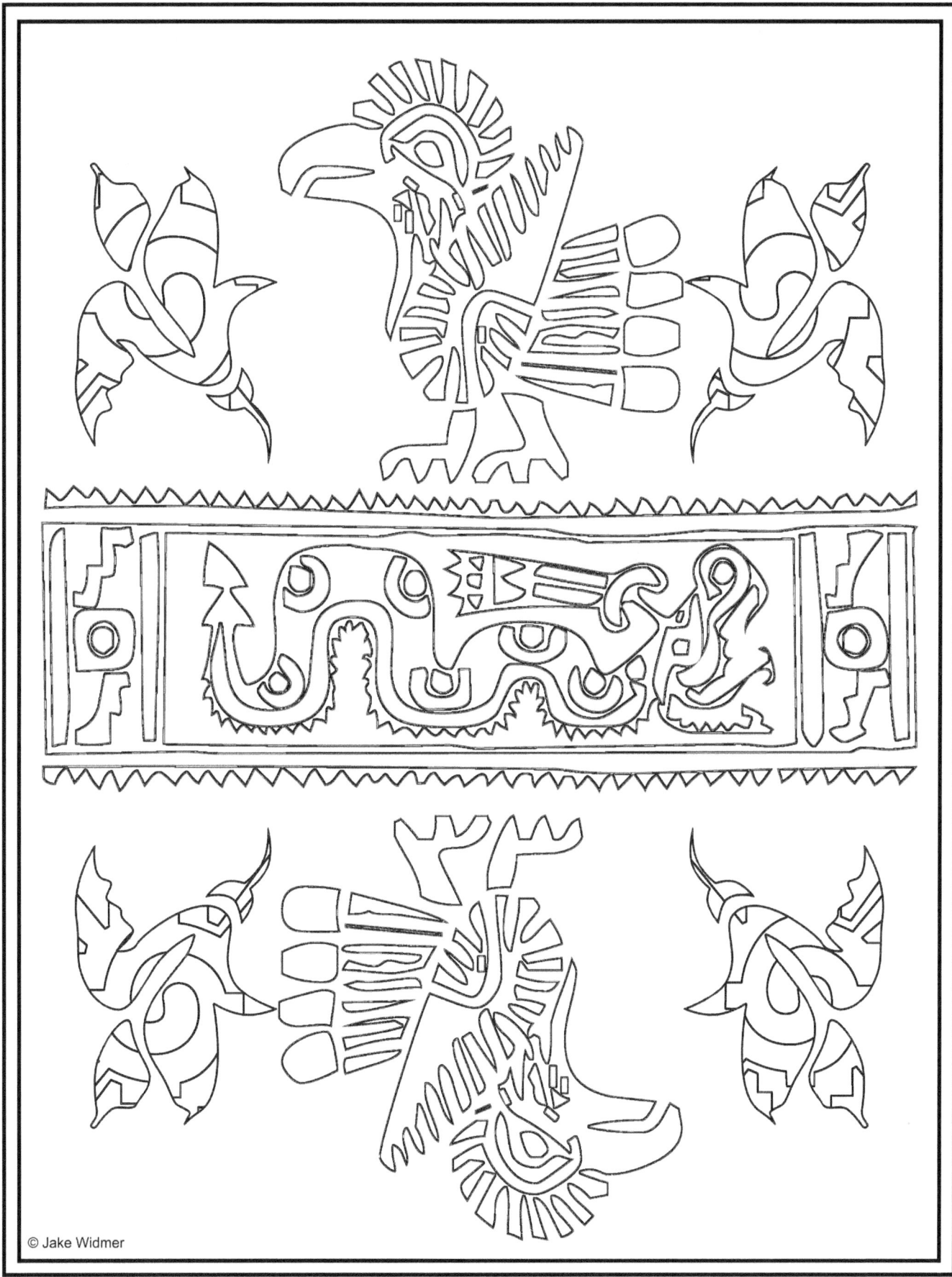

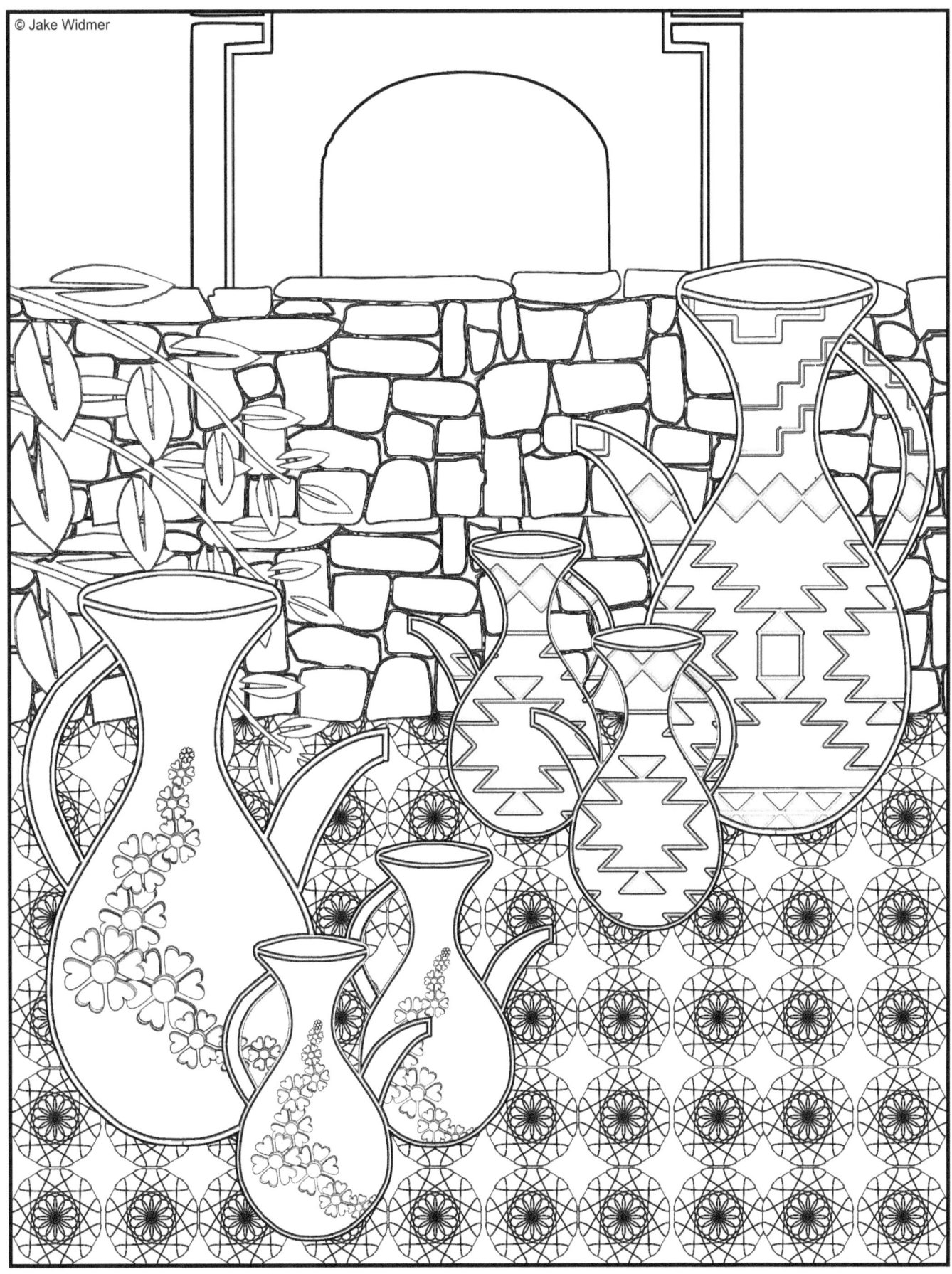
© Jake Widmer

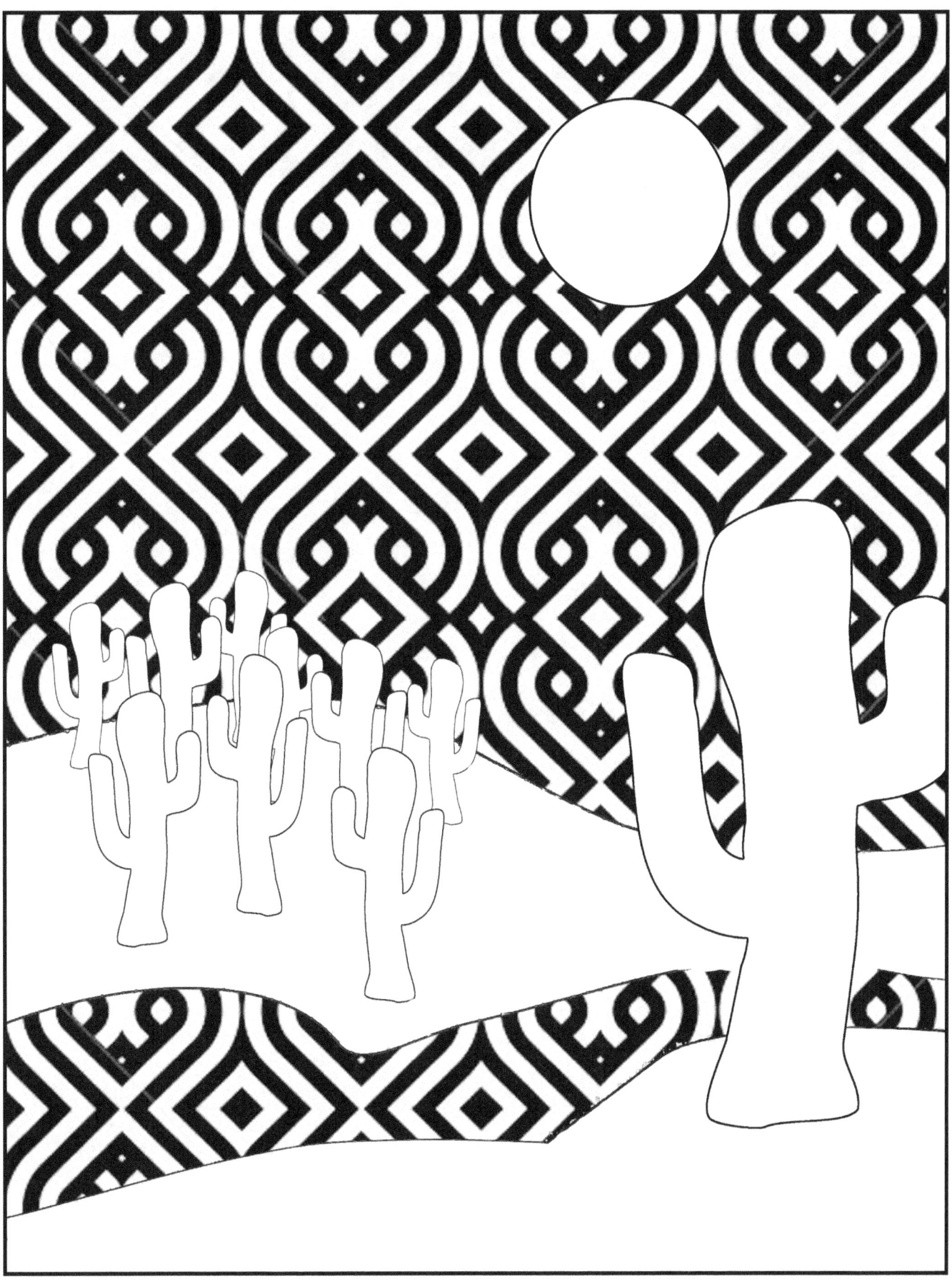

Clippee Coloring Books Wants to Thank You for Your Purchase

To Show Our Gratitude
We Would Like to Give You a Free Coloring Book Page Every Week

Just Go to Clippee **Coloring** and Subscribe to Join Our Private Facebook Group and You Can Download Past and Future Pages!!

Have an Amazing Day from Clippee! And Dont Forget to Confirm Your Email Address☺

<u>Clippee.com</u>

Other Books by Clippee Coloring

Tiki Hunt – Clippee.com/tikihunt

www.ingramcontent.com/pod-product-compliance
Lightning Source LLC
Chambersburg PA
CBHW080612180526
45168CB00007B/2880